Introducing Religions

Sikhism

Sue Penney

Heinemann LIBRARY

H www.heinemann.co.uk/library
Visit our website to find out more information about Heinemann Library books.

To order:
☎ Phone 44 (0) 1865 888066
🗎 Send a fax to 44 (0) 1865 314091
💻 Visit the Heinemann Bookshop at www.heinemann.co.uk/library to browse our catalogue and order online.

First published in Great Britain by Heinemann Library, Halley Court, Jordan Hill, Oxford OX2 8EJ, part of Harcourt Education.
Heinemann is a registered trademark of Harcourt Education Ltd.

Editorial: Clare Lewis
Design: Jo Hinton-Malivoire and Q2A Creative
Illustrations: Gecko Limited
Picture Research: Erica Newbury
Production: Helen McCreath

Printed in China by WKT.

13 digit ISBN 978 0 431 06656 1 (HB)
10 09 08 07 06
10 9 8 7 6 5 4 3 2 1

13 digit ISBN 978 0 481 06663 9 (PB)
11 10 09 08 07
10 9 8 7 6 5 4 3 2 1

British Library Cataloguing in Publication Data
Penney, Sue
Sikhism (Introducing Religions – 2nd edition)
294.6
A full catalogue record for this book is available from the British Library.

Acknowledgements
The publishers would like to thank the following for permission to reproduce photographs:
Alamy/Ark Religion pp. 8, 37; Alamy/Sally & Richard Greenhill p. 38; Andes Press Agency pp. 13, 23; 30, 46; Mohamed Ansar/Impact Photos p. 25; Circa Photo Library pp. 12, 44, 45; Mary Evans Picture Library p. 27; Sally and Richard Greenhill p. 11; Robert Harding Picture Library p. 28; Judy Harrison/Format Partners pp. 35, 41; The Hutchison Library pp. 14 (below), 20, 24, 42, 43, 49; Christine Osborne Pictures pp. 15, 16, 34, 36, 40, 48; Ann and Bury Peerless pp. 19, 21, 29, 31, 32, 33; Peter Sanders pp. 17, 47; World Religions p. 14.

The photograph on the previous page is reproduced by permission of Alamy/Yadid Levy.

Cover photograph of a young Sikh, reproduced with permission of Alamy/ Fredrik Renander.

The publishers would like to thank Dr Kanwaljit Kaur for her assistance in the preparation of this book.

Every effort has been made to contact copyright holders of any material reproduced in this book. Any omissions will be rectified in subsequent printings if notice is given to the publishers.

Contents

Words that are printed in bold, **like this**, are explained in the glossary on page 50.

MAP: where the main religions began

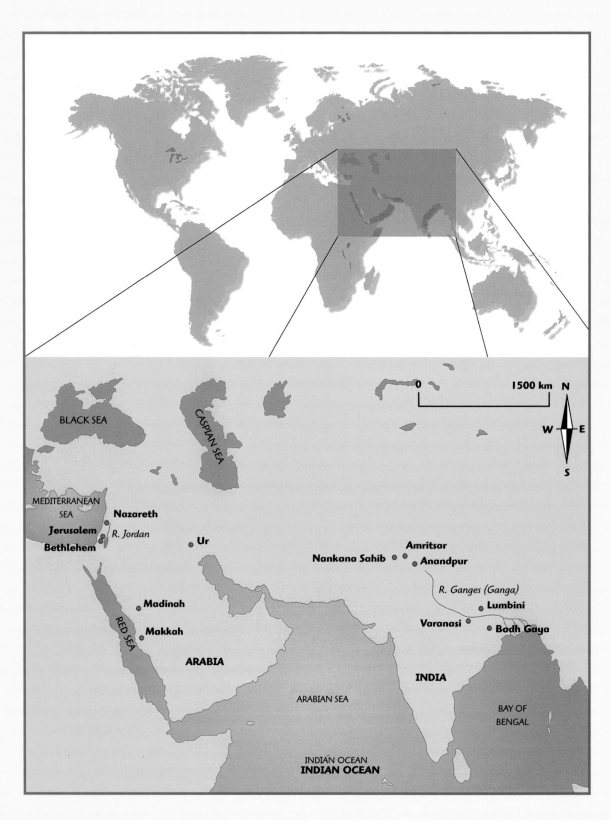

TIMECHART: when the main religions began

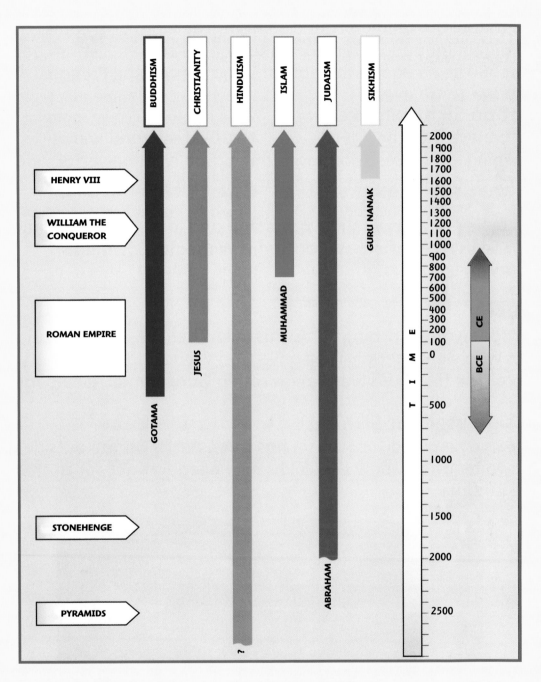

BUDDHISM
CHRISTIANITY
HINDUISM
ISLAM
JUDAISM
SIKHISM

HENRY VIII

WILLIAM THE CONQUEROR

GURU NANAK

ROMAN EMPIRE

MUHAMMAD

JESUS

T I M E

2000
1900
1800
1700
1600
1500
1400
1300
1200
1100
1000
900
800
700
600
500
400
300
200
100
0

500

1000

1500

2000

2500

CE

BCE

GOTAMA

STONEHENGE

ABRAHAM

PYRAMIDS

?

Note about dating systems *In this book dates are not called BC and AD, which is the Christian dating system. The letters BCE and CE are used instead. BCE stands for "Before the Common Era" and CE stands for "Common Era". BCE and CE can be used by people of all religions, Christians too. The year numbers are not changed.*

Introducing Sikhism

This section tells you about who Sikhs are.

Sikhs follow the religion called Sikhism. The word Sikh comes from the **Punjabi** language. It means a learner or seeker. Sikhism began about 500 years ago in the part of India we call the Punjab.

What do Sikhs believe?

Sikhs believe that there is one God. This God sees and knows everything, and cares about everything. God is all-powerful, and is **eternal**. That means God was never born and will never die.

Sikhs believe that they should **worship** and love God. The name which Sikhs most often use for God is **Waheguru**. It means Wonderful Lord.

Gurus

Sikhs follow the teachings of **Gurus**. Sikhs believe in 10 human Gurus who were special. They gave God's teachings to ordinary people. The first Guru was a man called Guru Nanak. (See page 18.)

The sign used for Sikhism

The sign often used for Sikhism has three parts. On the outside are two swords. These show that Sikhs may need to fight for truth and what is right.

The sign used for Sikhism

Between the swords is a circle. This reminds Sikhs that there is one God, and God has no beginning and no end, like a circle. In the middle is a two-edged sword called a **khanda**. This is a sign of God's power.

Another sign which Sikhs often use is made from letters. The letters mean "There is only one God".

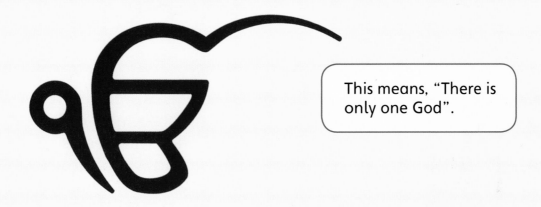

This means, "There is only one God".

Describing God

Sikhs usually use the name Waheguru for God. Sometimes they use the name Satnam, which means "eternal reality". This shows that they believe God has always been real. Sikhs never talk about God as "He" or "She", This is because they believe that God is a spirit, and is not male or female. They believe that God made people to be male and female, but it is wrong to talk about God as being either of these things. Guru Nanak said that God is "neither a man nor a woman".

Guru Nanak also said that God is "our mother and father". Sikhs believe that this shows how God cares about everything. They believe that in return people should care about God. Being careful about how they describe God is a way of reminding Sikhs how important God is.

The five Ks

This section tells you about special things Sikhs wear.

All full members of the Sikh religion wear five things which show they are Sikhs. In **Punjabi**, their names all begin with "K". So they are called the five Ks. Wearing the five Ks was begun by the 10th Guru, Guru Gobind Singh.

Kachera
Kachera are short trousers, worn as underwear. They were different from the long loose clothes that people often wore at that time.

Kara
The kara is a narrow bracelet made of steel. Sikhs wear it on their right wrist. It reminds them of God. The bracelet is a circle. Like a circle, God has no beginning and no end. The steel is strong. It reminds Sikhs that they must be strong when they are standing up for what is right.

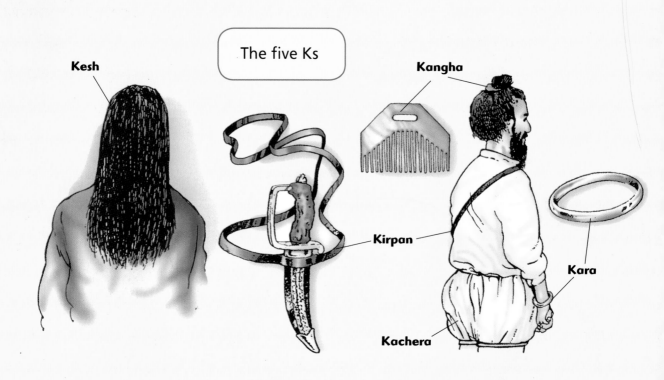

Kesh

The five Ks

Kangha

Kirpan

Kara

Kachera

A Sikh boy wearing a turban and the five Ks

Kesh

Kesh means hair. Guru Gobind Singh said that it should never be cut. For men, this also means not shaving.

Kangha

The kangha is a small comb worn in the hair. For Sikhs, being clean and tidy is important. Keeping their hair clean and tidy reminds them that their lives should be tidy and organized, too.

Kirpan

The kirpan is a sword. It reminds Sikhs that they should fight for what is right. It must never be used for attacking people. Most Sikhs today carry a short sword, which is kept in a special case with a strap.

The turban

A turban is a long piece of cloth which is wound round the head. It is not one of the five Ks, but wearing it is important for many male and some female Sikhs. Other men in India wear turbans, but it is a religious requirement for Sikh men.

A turban is wound round so that it covers the head completely. It helps to keep a Sikh's uncut hair tidy. Many Sikh families have a turban-tying ceremony for Sikh boys at about the age of 10. This is the age when boys wear a turban for the first time. A Sikh man should not wear any other cap or hat on his head.

The gurdwara

This section tells you about the place where Sikhs worship.

The Sikh place of **worship** is called a **gurdwara**. This is a **Punjabi** word which means "**Guru**'s door". It is a way of saying that the gurdwara is God's house.

A gurdwara does not have to be in a special building. The important thing is that the Guru Granth Sahib is there. This is the **holy** book of the Sikhs. (See pages 16–17.)

Outside the gurdwara

Some gurdwaras may be specially built. Others are in buildings which have been changed so that they can be used as a gurdwara. All gurdwaras have the yellow Sikh flag flying outside. The flag is called the **Nishan Sahib**.

Inside the gurdwara: the worship room

All gurdwaras have a room where people can meet for worship. Worship means praying to God, singing **hymns**, and asking for God's help in your life.

The worship room usually has a carpet or rugs on the floor, but there are no seats. The people sit on the floor. This shows that everyone is equal. It is also a way of showing respect for the Guru Granth Sahib. The Guru Granth Sahib is on a special throne at one end of the room. The throne is called a **takht**. It is the same sort of throne that a human Guru would sit on, and shows the same respect. In front of the takht is a place where people can leave gifts.

A gurdwara in Britain

Other rooms

If the gurdwara is large enough, it has a small room where the Guru Granth Sahib is kept when it is not being used in the worship room.

Most gurdwaras have another room where people can eat the **langar**. A kitchen for preparing the langar is also necessary.

Near the entrance to the gurdwara are places where people can leave their shoes. No one wears shoes in the worship room.

A takht

The langar

The langar is the meal which always ends Sikh meetings for worship. Eating together like this was begun by Guru Nanak, the first Guru. He said that it was very important because it shows that everyone is equal. At the time when Guru Nanak was alive, different groups of people in India were not allowed to eat together.

The meal is always the sort of food which would be eaten in the Punjab. It is cooked and served by both men and women. It is given free to everyone. The money to pay for it comes from gifts.

Worship in the gurdwara

This section tells you about how Sikhs worship in the gurdwara.

Sikhs do not have a special day when they go to the gurdwara. Many gurdwaras are open all day, every day, and people can call in to pray whenever they like. There are main **services** in the morning and at night.

A Sikh service

Before people go into the **worship** room, they take off their shoes and cover their heads. When they go into the worship room, the people go to the front and bow or kneel in front of the Guru Granth Sahib. When they go to sit down, they stay facing the front, because it is rude to turn their back on the Guru Granth Sahib. Men and women usually sit on different sides.

Worship in the gurdwara

Services in a gurdwara are usually held in **Punjabi**. They can last up to five hours, but people are not expected to stay the whole time. They can arrive after the beginning or leave before the end.

Services praise God, and there are readings and singing of poems from the Guru Granth Sahib. There are talks which explain the readings. The services are led by a man or a woman, who is called a **Granthi**.

It is the Granthi's job to read from the Guru Granth Sahib, and so he or she sits behind it, facing the rest of the people.

Musicians at a Sikh service

The Ardas

Sometimes the Granthi waves a special fan called a **chauri**. The chauri is made from yak hair or synthetic hair. It is the sort of fan which used to be waved over kings in India. Now the chauri is used to show respect to the Guru Granth Sahib.

Karah parshad

All Sikh services end with everyone being given a piece of special pudding called **karah parshad**. This is a sweet mixture of flour, sugar, and butter. Just before it is served, it is stirred with a kirpan (see page 11). Giving it to everyone and eating it together is another way of showing that everyone is equal.

The Ardas

The Ardas is the prayer that ends all Sikh services. It takes about five minutes. Everyone stands up. The person who is leading the prayer stands at the front, facing the Guru Granth Sahib. The prayer reminds everyone to remember God, and the 10 Gurus. It also reminds them that it is part of their duty as Sikhs to pass on the teachings of the Guru Granth Sahib to other people.

The Ardas asks God to look after all Sikhs and everyone in the world. If someone from the gurdwara is ill, prayers for that person will be included in the Ardas.

The Guru Granth Sahib

This section tells you about the holy book of the Sikhs.

The Guru Granth Sahib is used in all Sikh **worship**. Weddings take place in front of it, and babies are named using it. It always takes the most important place in the worship room. Having a Guru Granth Sahib is what makes a building a gurdwara.

The Guru Granth Sahib

The Guru Granth Sahib is a collection of **hymns**. A hymn is a special sort of poem which is used in worship.

Guru Nanak, the first Guru, wrote 974 hymns in the Guru Granth Sahib. Other hymns were written by other Gurus. There are also some hymns written by holy men who were **Hindus** and **Muslims**. Their ideas were similar to the ideas of the Sikh Gurus. The Guru Granth Sahib was completed by the 10th Guru in 1706. Since then, nothing has been added or taken away.

For nearly 200 years, all copies of the Guru Granth Sahib were carefully written out by hand. In 1852, a group of important Sikhs had a meeting and decided that they would allow copies to be printed for the first time. They also agreed that every copy should be exactly the same.

Taking the covers off the Guru Granth Sahib.

This is the reason why today every copy of the Guru Granth Sahib has the same number of pages – 1,430. A hymn in one copy is always found on the same page in any other copy.

Reading the Guru Granth Sahib

Some Sikhs have a copy of the Guru Granth Sahib at home.

Sikhs believe that it is so important that it should not be kept with other books. It should have a room of its own. This room then becomes a gurdwara, because the Guru Granth Sahib is there.

Gutkas

All Sikhs have smaller books called **Gutkas**. Gutkas contain hymns taken from the Guru Granth Sahib, and other prayers that Sikhs say every day. Sikhs treat Gutkas with great care, too.

How to treat the Guru Granth Sahib

When it is being used, the Guru Granth Sahib is put on the **takht**, the special throne at the front of the worship room. While it is open, there is always somebody sitting behind it to take care of it. When it is closed, it is covered with special cloths.

If the gurdwara is large enough, the Guru Granth Sahib is put away at night in a room of its own. There is a ceremony to "put it to rest" and another one to return it to the worship room the next morning. Carrying it is a great honour. It is always carried on the person's head. Sikhs treat it so carefully because they believe it is the word of God.

Guru Nanak

This section tells you about the first Sikh Guru.

Nanak was born in 1469 CE in a small village in India. The stories say that he was a special baby.

When he was a child, he was very interested in religion. His family were **Hindu**, but Nanak did not agree with everything that Hinduism taught.

When he grew up, Nanak went to work in an office. The people in the office were Muslims. Nanak talked to them about what they believed, too.

When he was about 30 years old, Nanak disappeared.

His friends thought that he must have drowned in the river. After three days, he came back to the village. Everyone was very pleased that he was not dead.

Nanak told the people that he had had a **vision** in which he had seen God. God had told him to teach people that they should live in a truthful way. They should treat all people as God's children.

After this time, Nanak was called **Guru** Nanak. He spent many years travelling around India and other countries teaching people.

This map shows the four journeys that Guru Nanak made.

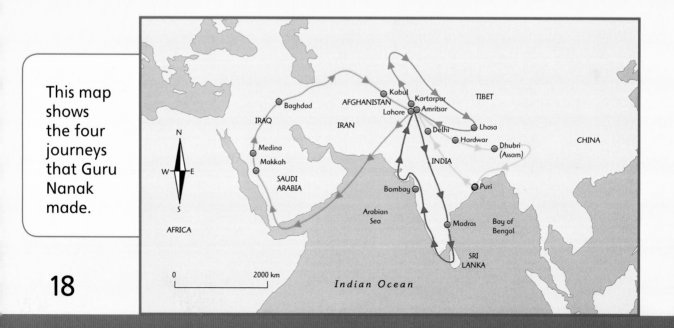

Guru Nanak

When he was an old man, Guru Nanak settled down in a village in northern India. A group of people came to live nearby. They wanted to learn more about what Guru Nanak was teaching. They became known as Sikhs because Sikh means "someone who wants to learn".

These people met for **worship**, and **meditated** together. Guru Nanak taught the people about God and about the right way to live. One of the men who came to learn was called Lehna.

Before Guru Nanak died, he chose Lehna to be the next Guru. He gave him a new name. He called him Angad. Angad means "part of me". Guru Nanak died in 1539 CE.

What Guru Nanak taught

· There is only one God. Worship and pray only to the one God.
· Different religions are different paths to the same one God.
· All humans are children of the same one God.
· Remember God, work hard, and help others.
· Men and women are all equal before God.
· Be kind to people, animals, and birds.
· Always speak the truth.

19

Other Sikh Gurus (1)

This section tells you about the three Gurus who came after Guru Nanak.

After **Guru** Nanak there were nine other Gurus. Sikhs say that all the Gurus thought in the same way. They say that they were like candles that have all been lit from the same flame. Each of the Gurus helped to make the new religion of Sikhism more organized.

Guru Angad (1539–1552)

Guru Angad was chosen by Guru Nanak. His most important work was writing down the **hymns** which Guru Nanak had written.

In those days, many people could not read or write. Guru Angad wanted to write down the hymns, but there was a problem. The people spoke **Punjabi**, but no one had ever written it down. Guru Angad worked out a way of writing Punjabi. It was called **Gurmukhi**. It is the language in which all the Sikh **holy** books are written.

Guru Amar Das (1552–1574)

Before he died, Guru Angad chose one of his Sikhs as the next Guru. He was called Guru Amar Das. He chose 22 Sikh men and women to be **missionaries** and tell people about the teachings of Guru Nanak.

Guru Amar Das asked all Sikhs to come to a big meeting twice a year, in the town where the Guru lived. This meant that he could meet them all himself. Guru Amar Das also continued Guru Nanak's teaching about how important it was that everyone should eat together.

The Guru Granth Sahib is written in Gurmukhi.

The Golden Temple at Amritsar

Guru Ram Das (1574–1581)

Guru Ram Das was chosen by Guru Amar Das. He decided that Sikhs should have a city which could be the centre of their faith. So he began building the city of Amritsar, which is in the Punjab in northern India.

Guru Ram Das also wrote the Sikh wedding hymns which Sikhs still use at their weddings.

Choosing a Guru

There is a story that Guru Nanak's sons thought one of them should be the next Guru. But Guru Nanak set them a test. He dropped a cup into a ditch full of muddy water. Then he asked for someone to go and get it.

His sons refused. They thought the Guru's sons were too good to do a job like that. But Lehna (Guru Angad) jumped into the water straight away without even being asked. Guru Nanak said that he should be the next Guru. He had shown that he knew caring for other people was important.

Other Sikh Gurus (2)

This section tells you about the later Sikh Gurus.

Guru Arjan (1581–1606)
Guru Arjan was the son of Guru Ram Das. He carried on the building at Amritsar begun by his father. He built a **gurdwara** in the middle of a lake there. This is now the Golden Temple. It is the most important building in the Sikh religion.

Guru Har Gobind (1606–1644)
Guru Har Gobind was Guru Arjan's son. He showed the Sikhs that they needed to fight for what they believed. Because of this, he was put in prison.

Then the ruler of India decided to let the Guru go free. The Guru refused to leave until 52 Hindu rulers who were also in the prison were allowed out, too. Sikhs remember this story every year (see page 35).

Guru Har Rai (1644–1661)
Guru Har Rai was Guru Har Gobind's grandson. He opened hospitals where medicine and treatment were given free to all.

Guru Har Krishan (1661–1664)
Guru Har Krishan was the son of Guru Har Rai. Even though he was very young, he cared about other people. He died when he was only eight years old, after he had helped to look after people suffering from smallpox.

Guru Tegh Bahadur (1664–1675)
Guru Tegh Bahadur was Guru Har Gobind's son. He was killed by the country's rulers because he refused to give up what he believed. His story is on page 32.

Guru Gobind Singh (1675–1708)
Guru Gobind Singh began the **Khalsa**. Khalsa means the pure ones. It is the name for Sikhs who are full members of the religion (see page 24).

Guru Gobind Singh

Before Guru Gobind Singh died, he said that he was not going to choose a new human Guru. From then on, the Sikhs' Guru would be their **holy** book. This is why it is called the Guru Granth Sahib.

How Guru Gobind Singh chose the Guru Granth Sahib

When Guru Gobind Singh was dying, he asked to be taken to the room where the holy book was kept. At that time the holy book was called the Adi Granth, which means "first book". Guru Gobind Singh bowed his head in front of it to show respect. Then he spoke to the people with him.

He said: "My spirit lives on in the Khalsa and the Guru Granth Sahib. Obey the Guru Granth Sahib. Let anyone who wishes to meet me search its **hymns**." He had shown the Sikhs that in future their Guru should be the Guru Granth Sahib. Granth means "a big book". Sahib is a word used to show respect.

The Khalsa

This section tells you about how the Khalsa began.

What is the Khalsa?

The **Khalsa** is the name given to Sikhs who are full members of the Sikh religion. The name Khalsa means "the pure ones".

The Khalsa was begun by Guru Gobind Singh in 1699. He said that being a member of the Khalsa was more important than anything else. He told the people to do two things to show that they were members.

The first thing people had to do was to drink **amrit** from the same bowl. Amrit is a mixture of sugar and water. In those days people who came from different groups or religions never ate or drank together. Drinking the amrit together showed that they cared more about being Sikhs than they did about where they came from.

These men are dressed like the Panj Piare, the first members of the Khalsa.

The other thing people had to do was share a name. Guru Gobind Singh said that all men should take the name of **Singh**. Singh means lion.

All the women should take the name of **Kaur**. Kaur means princess. People who share the same name are part of the same family, so sharing these names shows that all Sikhs are part of the family of Sikhism. Since that day, all Sikhs have used these names as part of their own name.

Preparing for the amrit ceremony

The amrit ceremony

The **amrit ceremony** is the special ceremony where people join the Khalsa. Apart from the people who are joining, only people who are already members may take part. Everyone wears the five Ks.

The ceremony is led by five people, to remember the Panj Piare, the five men who offered to give their lives to Guru Gobind Singh. One of the five leaders repeats the duties which members of the Khalsa must keep. There are prayers and readings from the Guru Granth Sahib.

The people who are joining, kneel on their right knee. They drink some amrit, then some is sprinkled on their eyes, hair, and hands. There are more prayers, then everyone shares **karah parshad**. After this ceremony, Sikhs are expected to keep all the duties of the religion.

How the Khalsa began

Guru Gobind Singh called a meeting of all the Sikhs. He asked if there was anyone who was ready to die for what they believed. No one answered. He asked this question two more times. One man came forward. Guru Gobind Singh took the man into his tent. Then he came out with his sword covered in blood! He asked the question again. Another man came forward. The same thing happened. Altogether five men were taken away.

Then the Guru went into his tent and came back with all five men. The Guru called them the five beloved ones (Panj Piare), and said they would be the first members of the Khalsa.

25

Sikh history

This section tells you about what happened to Sikhism after the 10 Gurus.

After the death of Guru Gobind Singh, the Sikhs had a very difficult time. India had been taken over, and the new rulers of the country wanted everyone to join their religion. People who did not obey were punished. For about 100 years, anyone who was a Sikh was in danger of being killed, just because they were Sikhs. Many Sikhs were killed, and others went into hiding. They organized secret armies to try to fight the rulers.

Ranjit Singh

Then a young soldier became a leader in the Sikh army. He was called Ranjit Singh. He lived from 1780 until 1839. He became the leader of a group of Sikhs after his father died. This was when Ranjit was only 12 years old.

Although Ranjit Singh was very young, he was a very good soldier and leader. The army began winning battles, and Sikhs began to have lands of their own. Ranjit Singh became the ruler of a huge Empire. It included the Punjab and most of what today we know as northern India.

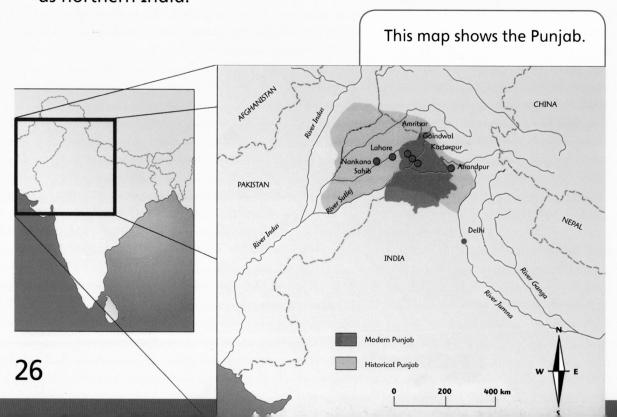

This map shows the Punjab.

Ranjit Singh

Ranjit Singh ruled for 40 years. Many Sikhs think of this as the best time Sikhs have ever had.

Ranjit Singh died in 1839, and in 1849 the British took over India. Sikhs still had many difficulties. For example, they were not allowed to run **gurdwaras** themselves. Sikh leaders had to work hard to make Sikhism a separate religion again.

It was not until 1909 that laws were passed allowing Sikhs in India to hold marriage services in gurdwaras. This was an important change. After it, laws were passed which meant that Sikhs could follow their religion in their own way.

Today, there are about 19 million Sikhs in the world. About 15 million Sikhs live in India, mainly in the area of northern India called the Punjab.

Outside of India, the largest group of Sikhs is in Britain, where about 400,000 Sikhs live.

A separate country for Sikhs

Most Sikhs have always lived in the area of India called the Punjab. When the British left India in 1947, the Punjab was divided. One-third of it stayed in India, the other two-thirds became part of the new country of Pakistan.

Many Sikhs lost their homes and land. Thousands of people were killed in riots. Since then, many thousands more Sikhs have been killed. Many Sikhs are asking for a separate country of their own, which they would call Khalistan.

Sikh holy places

This section tells you about places which Sikhs believe are important for their religion.

Amritsar

Amritsar is the most important place for Sikhs. It is the city which was begun by **Guru** Ram Das. The most important building is the **gurdwara** called the Golden Temple, which was built by Guru Arjan. This is built on an island in the middle of a lake. It was built with doors on all four sides, to show that people from all parts of the world are welcome there.

It is made of marble, and the top half is covered in a thin layer of gold. The walls are covered with verses from the Guru Granth Sahib.

Readings from the Guru Granth Sahib start at three o'clock every morning, and go on until 10 o'clock at night. Then a procession of people takes the Guru Granth Sahib from the **worship** room to the room where it is kept for the night. It is carried back the next morning. Taking part in this procession is very important for Sikhs.

Other important places

Most of the other important places for Sikhs are where the Gurus were born or died.

The lake and the Golden Temple at Amritsar

A gurdwara at Anandpur

Nankana Sahib

Nankana Sahib is the town where Guru Nanak was born and grew up. Its name was changed so that it remembers the Guru. There are many **gurdwaras** in the town.

Anandpur

Anandpur is in the north of India. It is the town where Guru Gobind Singh began the Khalsa. It is also the place where the head of Guru Tegh Bahadur was brought to be **cremated**. There is a gurdwara at the place where the head was cremated.

Sikhs and pilgrimage

All religions have places that are important to people who follow that religion. Many people like to visit these places. A journey to visit a place that is important in your religion is called a pilgrimage. Sikhism is different from most other religions, because the Gurus said that Sikhs should not go on pilgrimages. Guru Nanak said that the way you live is more important than places you visit. He said, "The thief remains a thief even if he bathes at a place of pilgrimage."

Sikh festivals

This section tells you about two of the most important Sikh festivals.

The most important Sikh festivals remember the birth or the death of a **Guru**. In **Punjabi** they are called **Gurpurbs**.

The most important part of a gurpurb is a reading of the Guru Granth Sahib from beginning to end without stopping. This is called an **Akhand Path**.

Akhand Path

An Akhand Path takes about 48 hours.

It is always timed to end early in the morning of the day of the festival. While the reading is going on, Sikhs make a special effort to go to the **gurdwara**. They listen and meditate. **Langar** is always served as the reading is taking place.

Guru Nanak's birthday

Sikhs all over the world celebrate the birthday of Guru Nanak in November every year. There are often processions through the streets. Five people usually lead the procession, to remind Sikhs of the five men who were the first to join the **Khalsa**.

The five wear yellow robes with a wide blue belt, and yellow turbans, because this is what the first five men wore.

Reading the Guru Granth Sahib at an Akhand Path

A Gurpurb procession

Next in the procession comes a lorry or open truck which carries the Guru Granth Sahib on its throne. This is beautifully decorated with flowers and banners. The people in the procession sing **hymns** from the Guru Granth Sahib. People watching the procession are often given sweets to remember that Guru Nanak said all people should be able to eat together.

The birthday of Guru Gobind Singh
This Gurpurb takes place on 5 January. It is celebrated in the same way as the birthday of Guru Nanak.

The most important procession is in the town of Patna in India. This is the town where the Guru was born.

How an Akhand Path is organized
An Akhand Path is a reading of the Guru Granth Sahib all the way through. The reading can be done by any man or woman who can read **Gurmukhi** well enough to be able to read it clearly in front of lots of people. People take it in turns, but no one ever reads for more than two hours at a time. This is so that they do not get tired. There is always a reserve reader in case someone is ill.

Before going to the gurdwara, the reader has a bath, and before starting to read they wash their hands. This is to make sure that they are clean to touch the Guru Granth Sahib, and because they think it is so important.

Other festivals

This section tells you about the Gurpurbs that remember the martyrdom of two Sikh Gurus.

The martyrdom of Guru Arjan

Guru Arjan was the first Sikh to be killed because of what he believed. Someone who dies because of their religion is called a **martyr**, so their death is called a martyrdom. Guru Arjan was killed because he refused to change his religion to the religion of the country's ruler.

Sikhs remember Guru Arjan's death on 6 June. They give cool drinks to passers-by to remember the torture of the Guru.

The martyrdom of Guru Tegh Bahadur

Guru Tegh Bahadur's death is remembered on 24 November every year. It is especially important in Delhi, the capital of India. This is where he was killed. There is a beautiful **gurdwara** at the place where he died. Sikhs go there to **worship** as part of the **Gurpurb**.

In India at that time **Hindus** and Sikhs were being killed.

This was because they would not change their religion. Important Hindus came to see Guru Tegh Bahadur, to ask his advice.

A gurpurb procession, remembering Guru Tegh Bahadur

This gurdwara was built where Guru Tegh Bahadur was killed.

The Guru said everyone should be able to worship in the way they felt was right. He went to speak to the Emperor (the ruler of India), who offered the Guru all sorts of good things if he would change his religion. But the Guru refused. The Emperor ordered that the Guru should have his head cut off.

Sikhs believe that this was very important. If Guru Tegh Bahadur had given in, Hindus as well as Sikhs would have had to give up what they believed.

Guru Tegh Bahadur

There is a Sikh story which shows that even when Guru Tegh Bahadur was a baby, he was always unusual. The story says that when Tegh Bahadur was born, he was taken to his father, Guru Har Gobind. Guru Har Gobind always wore two swords. This was to show that Sikhs need to fight in two ways – they need to fight for what is right as well as for religious truth.

When Guru Har Gobind took his son in his arms, the baby reached out and held on to one of the swords. This is why his father chose the name Tegh Bahadur, which means "master of the sword".

Melas

This section tells you about the Sikh festivals called melas.

Melas means fairs. There are many melas in different towns in India, celebrating things that happened there. This section looks at two important melas which are celebrated all over the world.

Baisakhi

Baisakhi is a spring festival. It falls on 13 or 14 April. It is a popular time for holding the **amrit ceremony**.

This is because Baisakhi remembers the time when **Guru** Gobind Singh began the **Khalsa** in 1699. (See pages 24–25.)

At Baisakhi there are services in the gurdwara. The services begin soon after dawn. These may last all day, with people coming and going, leaving when they have stayed as long as they can.

The **langar** is served all day. There are readings from the Guru Granth Sahib, and talks that remind people of the first Baisakhi and how important it was.

Replacing the Nishan Sahib at Baisakhi

At Baisakhi the **Nishan Sahib** is always changed. This is the Sikh flag which flies outside every gurdwara. It is taken down, and the flagpole is cleaned. The yellow covers for the flagpole and flag are replaced.

Divali

Divali means festival of lights. It takes place in November. It is an important festival for **Hindus** as well as Sikhs, but they celebrate it in different ways.

Sikhs remember it as the time when Guru Har Gobind was released from prison in 1619. The people in Amritsar were so pleased to see him that they lit lamps in every house to welcome him home.

Lighting candles at Divali

Like other festivals, Divali is often celebrated with bonfires and firework displays.

A Divali story

At Divali, Sikhs remember that Guru Har Gobind cared about others. The Emperor said he could leave prison, but the Guru said that 52 Hindu princes must be allowed to go, too. The Emperor said that only the princes who could hold onto the Guru's cloak could go, and he must leave through a narrow gate. It was only wide enough for one man. The Guru had long cords fastened to his cloak, so everyone could hold on. All the princes were freed.

Sewa

This section tells you about how Sikhs believe they should help other people.

Sewa is a very important idea for Sikhs. It means service – helping others. Sikhs believe that helping others is part of the way they can **worship** God.

Sewa is not just helping other Sikhs. The important thing is to offer help to anyone who needs it, no matter who they are.

Sewa may mean giving money to help people who are very poor. **Guru** Gobind Singh said that if they could, Sikhs should give one-tenth of any money they have earned so that it can be used to help other people. But Sikhs know that this is not always possible. Also, for people who have a lot of money, giving some of it away may not mean very much. Giving their time may be much harder.

There are many jobs that can be part of sewa. Cleaning the **gurdwara**, for example, or helping to cook or serve the **langar**.

Talking to people about what they believe about God can also be part of sewa, but Sikhs do not try to persuade people to become Sikhs. They think it is important that everyone serves God in the way they believe is right.

Serving the langar

Medicine

Sewa can also mean helping to look after people who are ill. Sikhs have always believed that caring for people who are ill is important. Guru Nanak spent a lot of his time with people who were ill, and so did many of the other Gurus.

A Sikh doctor in Britain

The eighth Guru, Guru Har Krishan, died because he was helping to look after people who had smallpox. Many Sikhs today become doctors or nurses.

In India, where most Sikhs live, many people are too poor to pay for medical care. Some Indian gurdwaras have special clinics where people can go to be given free treatment and medicines.

Why care about other people?

Sikhs believe that caring for everyone is an important part of their religion. They believe God loves everyone in exactly the same way, so no one is better than anyone else.

They also believe that you can only love God if you love other people.

Sikhism teaches that all people should be treated equally. There is a story that the third Guru, Guru Amar Das, was visited by the Emperor. The Emperor was very important, but Guru Amar Das still expected him to sit on the floor and eat the langar in the same way as everyone else.

Sikh life

This section tells you about some of the ways in which being a Sikh affects people's lives.

Everyday life

All Sikhs who are members of the **Khalsa** promise to try to live so that they are as much like the **Gurus** as possible. This means that they should work hard and earn their living honestly. They should not do any jobs which might hurt other people. Gambling and stealing are forbidden, and so is having affairs.

Sikhs should not take any drugs except proper medicines. They should not drink alcohol or smoke.

Sikhism does not have strict laws about food, except that no Sikh will eat meat from an animal which has been killed in a way they think is cruel. Many Sikhs do not eat beef, because they do not want to upset **Hindus**, who believe that cows are **holy**.

Many Sikhs spend time every day **meditating** and reading the holy books. The Guru Granth Sahib has been translated into several other languages.

A class at a gurdwara

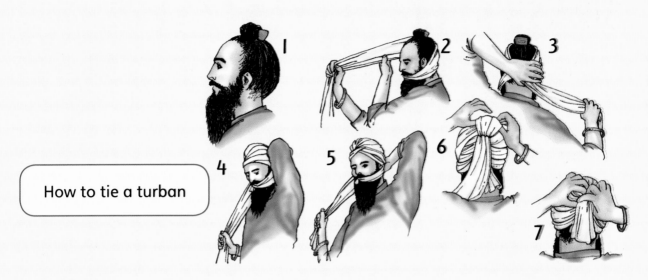

How to tie a turban

But many Sikhs choose to learn Gurmukhi so that they can read it in the language in which it was written.

Turbans

Today, wearing a turban is an important way of showing that someone is a Sikh. It has become a part of what Sikh men wear. A turban is a piece of material about five metres (16.5 feet) long which is wound around the head.

In India, important people once wore them as a sign that they were powerful. Guru Gobind Singh started to wear one to show that the Sikhs were powerful. Other Sikhs copied him. Sikh men should not wear anything else on their head.

The story of Bhai Lalo

Sikhs tell this story to show why you should live your life carefully. Guru Nanak once chose to visit a poor man called Bhai Lalo. A rich man was upset that Guru Nanak had not visited him instead.

Guru Nanak went to the rich man's house, and picked up a piece of bread. He squeezed it and drops of blood came out. Then he squeezed a piece of bread from Bhai Lalo's house. Drops of milk came out. Guru Nanak said that this showed that Bhai Lalo was honest, even though he was poor. The rich man had made his money by being unkind to other people.

The Sikh family

This section tells you about the way Sikhs live as a family.

In India, where many Sikh families come from, most people live in **extended families**. This means that the family all live together or near to one another. Cousins know each other as well as their brothers and sisters.

Sikhs believe that families are very important. They say that the best way for children to learn about the religion is for them to be taught about it at home, and learn from older relations. Children are taught that they must be polite to older people, and respect their opinions.

A Sikh family in Britain

Arranged marriages

Sikhs have always believed that part of the duty of the parents is to help their son or daughter choose a wife or husband. This is called an **arranged marriage**.

Marriage joins two families as well as the two people, so it is important that the person chosen is suitable. Years ago, things were very strict, and a couple would not meet before their wedding day. Today, a young person may suggest someone they know and like. They usually meet at least a few times before their wedding. A Sikh couple must agree to their marriage, or it cannot take place.

Women can lead worship.

Women in Sikhism

Guru Nanak said that women were just as good as men, and they should be treated in the same way. In those days, this was not usual. There are stories in Sikh history about women soldiers who have fought in battles for the Sikh religion.

In the **gurdwara**, men and women are treated the same. They take part in the same ceremonies, and women may become **Granthis** and lead **worship** in the gurdwara. **Karah parshad** and the **langar** are served and eaten by men and women together.

Teachings about women

At the time of the Gurus, most people thought that women were not as good as men. They were like possessions belonging to a family. When they married, they were given to another family. The Gurus' teachings about women were different.

Apart from Guru Har Krishan, who died when he was a child, all of them were married. This shows that they believed marriage and the family were important. Guru Nanak said that even the most powerful man had once been a baby with a mother, so women should be treated well. This is why Sikhism says that men and women should be treated equally.

Sikhs in other countries

This section tells you about Sikhs who live in countries other than India.

About 400,000 Sikhs live in Britain.

Most Sikhs still live in the area of India called the Punjab. In the last hundred years, many Sikhs have moved away from India. Many Sikhs now live in the United States, Australia, Canada, and East Africa, as well as countries in Europe and South America.

About 400,000 Sikhs live in Britain, probably more than any other country except India. In the United States there are about 200,000. There are about 8,000 Sikhs in Australia.

Gurdwaras

When Sikhs are living in a country where most people do not share their religion, the **gurdwara** is even more important. The first gurdwaras in other countries were usually in people's houses, or in a room or building which had been changed to become a gurdwara. As Sikhs became more at home, Gurdwaras began to be specially built. There are about 200 gurdwaras in Britain.

There is no particular day when Sikhs are expected to go to the gurdwara. In many countries Sunday has become a popular day, because it fits into the usual way of life. Gurdwaras have also become important places where Sikhs can meet and talk with other Sikhs.

These children are learning about Sikhism.

Converts

A **convert** is someone who has become a member of a religion, rather than being born one. Sikhs do not try to persuade other people to become Sikhs.

Sikhs believe that it is important to try to see God in everyone, no matter what religion they are. Some people do decide to convert to Sikhism, perhaps because they have learnt about the religion and agree with its teachings.

Visiting a gurdwara

Sikhs welcome people who are interested enough in their religion to want to go and visit a gurdwara. People who do visit are expected to behave properly, and should cover their head and take off their shoes. Short skirts or shorts would not be suitable clothing.

Anyone visiting a gurdwara should make sure that they are not carrying tobacco or anything which contains alcohol. If they go to a **service**, they should be prepared to share the **karah parshad**, and to stay for the langar. It would not be polite to refuse either.

Special occasions in childhood

This section tells you about special things that happen to young Sikhs.

Birth

As soon as possible after a baby has been born, someone repeats the first words of the **Guru** Granth Sahib. These words sum up the most important things that Sikhs believe. It means that the first thing the baby hears are the most important Sikh beliefs.

Friends and relations visit the baby soon after birth, and bring presents for the baby.

Parents often show how pleased they are about the birth of their baby by giving small presents, such as sweets, to friends and people who live near by.

The naming ceremony

The naming ceremony is to thank God for the baby's birth, and to choose its name. It is part of a normal service at the **gurdwara**. The ceremony usually takes place when the baby is a few weeks old.

Often the parents take a new **rumala** with them as a gift for the gurdwara. This is the cloth which is used for covering the Guru Granth Sahib when it is not being read.

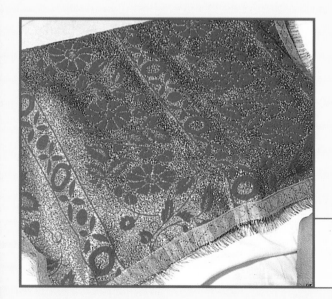

When a baby is being named, the Ardas prayer includes the names of the parents, and prayers for the baby. At the end of the prayer, the baby's parents go to the front of the gurdwara. The **Granthi** opens the Guru Granth Sahib without choosing a particular page.

A Guru Granth Sahib with its rumala

A naming ceremony

He or she reads the first new verse on the left-hand page. Then the Granthi tells the parents which letter began the first word.

The baby's parents then choose a name that begins with that letter. They tell the Granthi the name they have chosen, and the Granthi tells the people who are at the service. Everyone shouts "Sat sri akal", which means "God is truth". This shows that they agree.

Sometimes, after it has been given its name the baby is given amrit as well. This is not part of the religious ceremony.

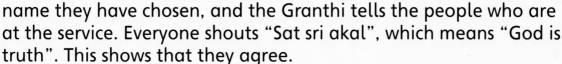

Sikh names

Sikhs do not have strict rules about names. The same name may be used for boys and girls. This means you can only tell if someone is a boy or girl by whether they use the name Singh or Kaur. This shows that women are equal to men.

Some Sikhs use Singh or Kaur as their last name. Others use it as their middle name followed by their family name. Girls do not usually use their father's or husband's name, because they use Kaur instead. Many Sikhs also have "pet names" which members of their family and close friends use, rather than the given name.

Marriage

This section tells you about Sikh marriage.

Sikhs believe that marriage is very important. Sikh weddings must take place in front of the **Guru** Granth Sahib. In Western countries this usually means that they take place in a **gurdwara**, but in India they are often held in the open air. Any Sikh may perform the marriage ceremony, if he or she has been chosen by both families.

The bridegroom usually wears a red or pink turban, and has a scarf round his neck. After bowing to the Guru Granth Sahib, he sits facing it. The bride's father puts a garland of flowers on the Guru Granth Sahib. The bride comes in with her sister or another female relation. They bow to the Guru Granth Sahib.

The bride sits next to the bridegroom. Her father puts a garland of flowers round her neck.

The marriage begins with prayers and readings from the Guru Granth Sahib. The person leading the **service** gives a talk about marriage and what it means. Then the bride's father puts the end of the bridegroom's scarf in her hand. She holds this for the rest of the ceremony.

The most important part of the marriage is the reading of the **Lavan**. This is a special wedding **hymn** written by Guru Ram Das.

People give the couple money.

A Sikh wedding

The Lavan has four verses. Each verse is spoken, then sung. As it is sung, the bride and groom walk around the Guru Granth Sahib. When they have done this for the fourth time, they are married. Everyone joins in the Ardas prayer, and shares **karah parshad**.

Divorce

Sikhs do not encourage divorce, but if the marriage cannot be saved, divorce is allowed. Either person may marry again in the gurdwara.

Sikh brides

Preparing for her wedding day is very important for a Sikh woman. For days before the wedding, friends, and relations visit the bride's house.

On the evening before the wedding, female friends and relations usually meet at the bride's house. They have a party and eat special sweet foods.

They paint patterns on the bride's hands and feet, using a special dye which takes several days to wear off. For the wedding itself, Sikh brides wear red, orange, or pink. They usually wear lots of beautiful gold jewellery, too.

Funerals

This section tells you about what happens when a Sikh dies.

What do Sikhs believe about death?

Sikhs believe that when you die, your **soul** moves on to another body. This cycle of dying and being born again happens over and over again. It goes on until, with God's help, you become close enough to God to break out of the cycle. Then you can go and live with God forever. **Guru** Nanak said that this belief explains why life can sometimes seem unfair. Things you have done in lives you have lived before can follow you. This can make a difference to what happens to you in this life.

Believing this makes a difference to what Sikhs believe about death. They say that it is like going to sleep. You go to sleep when you are tired, and wake up ready for another day. In the same way, you die, and are born again to a new life.

Of course, friends and relations are sad that the person they love is not with them any more. But Sikhism teaches them to remember that the person has gone on to another life.

Sikh funerals

After a Sikh has died, their body is washed and dressed in the five Ks. Then it is wrapped in a white sheet. Sikhs are always **cremated**, and the **funeral** takes place as soon as possible after death.

In India the body is placed on a special fire in the open air. Male relatives help to carry the body and lift it onto the fire. In Western countries, it is taken to a **crematorium**, and male relatives help to carry the coffin.

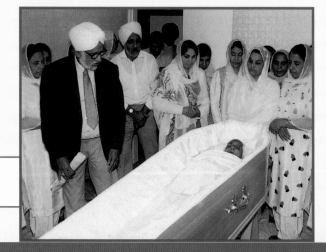

A Sikh funeral in Britain

Male relatives help to carry the coffin

The most important prayer at the funeral is the **Sohila**. This is the same prayer that Sikhs say every night. It reminds Sikhs that death is like sleep.

After the body has been burned, the ashes are scattered on a river or the sea. Sikhs do not put up gravestones. They say that a person should be remembered for the good things they have done in their life.

Guru Nanak's death

There is a story that when Guru Nanak was dying, Sikh friends who had been **Hindus** and **Muslims** came to see him. Hindus always cremate people who have died. Muslims always bury them. The Hindus wanted to burn Guru Nanak's body. The Muslims wanted him to say that it could be buried. Guru Nanak said they should cover his body with a cloth, then the Hindus should put flowers at one side, Muslims the other. The people whose flowers were still fresh in the morning could choose what to do.

Guru Nanak died, and his friends did as he said. In the morning, all the flowers were still fresh, but the body had gone! Sikhs say this story shows the soul is far more important than the body.

Glossary

Akhand Path non-stop reading of the Guru Granth Sahib from beginning to end

amrit ceremony ceremony in which people become members of the Khalsa

amrit special mixture of sugar and water, used in amrit ceremonies

arranged marriage marriage in which the partner is chosen or suggested by relations

chauri special fan waved over the Guru Granth Sahib

convert someone who has chosen to become a member of a religion rather than because their family are members

cremate to burn a dead body

crematorium place where dead bodies are burned

eternal lasting for ever

extended family grandparents, cousins, and other relations, living as one family

funeral service to remember someone who has died

Granthi person who leads Sikh services

gurdwara Sikh place of worship

Gurmukhi written form of the Punjabi language

gurpurb festival in honour of a Guru

Guru religious teacher (for Sikhs, one of 10 religious teachers)

Gutka book containing the most important Sikh hymns and the daily prayers

Hindu follower of the religion of Hinduism

holy to do with God

hymn kind of poem used in worship

karah parshad special food shared out at Sikh services

Kaur "princess", the name given to all Sikh females by Guru Gobind Singh

Khalsa full members of the Sikh religion

khanda two-edged sword

langar the free meal which is part of Sikh worship and the kitchen where it is prepared

Lavan wedding hymn written by Guru Ram Das

martyr someone who dies for what they believe

meditate think deeply, especially about religion

mela "fair" – Sikh festival

missionary someone who tells other people about their religion

Muslim follower of the religion of Islam

Nishan Sahib Sikh flag

Punjabi Indian language spoken by most Sikhs

rumala piece of cloth which is used for covering the Guru Granth Sahib when it is not being used

service meeting for worship

sewa service, helping others

Singh "lion", name given to all Sikh males by Guru Gobind Singh

Sohila Sikh night-time prayer

soul spirit that lives on after death

takht throne for the Guru Granth Sahib

vision special dream, usually to do with religion

Waheguru Sikh name for God

worship pray and give thanks to God

Find out more

More books to read
Ganeri, Anita. *Sacred texts: The Guru Granth Sahib and Sikhism*. London, Books for Children, 2003

Maryled, Jon. *Living religions: Sikhism*. Oxford, Heinemann Library, 2003

Penney, Sue. *World beliefs and cultures: Sikhism*. Oxford, Heinemann Library, 2001

Using the internet
You can find out more about Sikhism in books and on the Internet. Use a search engine such as **www.yahooligans.com** to search for information. A search for the word "Sikhism" will bring back lots of results, but it may be difficult to find the information you want. Try refining your search to look for some of the people and ideas mentioned in this book, such as "Guru Nanak" or "women in Sikhism".

Website
www.bbc.co.uk/religion/religions/sikhism/index
Try looking here for up-to-date information and articles on Sikhism and Sikhs.

Index